THE ALLISON CONTEMPORARY PIANO COLLECTION

Repertoire suitable for Auditions in the National Guild of Piano Teachers

Compiled and classified by
Julia Amada Kruger, Vice President of the American College of
Musicians/National Guild of Piano Teachers

Copyright 1996

by

Keyboard Creations
Austin, Texas
(A Division of Creative Music)

FOREWORD

We are pleased to provide teachers with a new and exciting format for piano literature expressly designed for Auditions in the National Guild of Piano Teachers. This series is a classified compilation of Guild members' works with appropriate Musicianship Phases and IMMT. We hope you will find this series extremely useful and a valuable addition to the Guild library.

I would like to offer my appreciation and thanks to those who donated their works to the project as well as those persons involved in its completion.

Richard Allison
President,
American College of Musicians,
National Guild of Piano Teachers

ACKNOWLEDGEMENT

Special acknowledgement and appreciation to Darryl Dunn of KeyNote
Productions; and to Joseph M. Martin; Austin, Texas

Photograph used by permission of the Yamaha Corporation

Use of this photograph does not constitute an endorsement
of the product by either the American College of Musicians/
National Guild of Piano Teachers or the publisher.

TABLE OF CONTENTS

IE CLASSIFICATION

IF CLASSIFICATION

MUSICIANSHIP PHASES

Willow Boughs

for John

Theresa Sauer Tisano

A Major (hands together)
(see Syllabus for metronomic requirement)

(hands together)

Root
Pos.

I   IV   I   V₇   I
                or V

Sometimes I Think I'm Dreaming

Lois Askren

D.C. al Coda

(Coda)

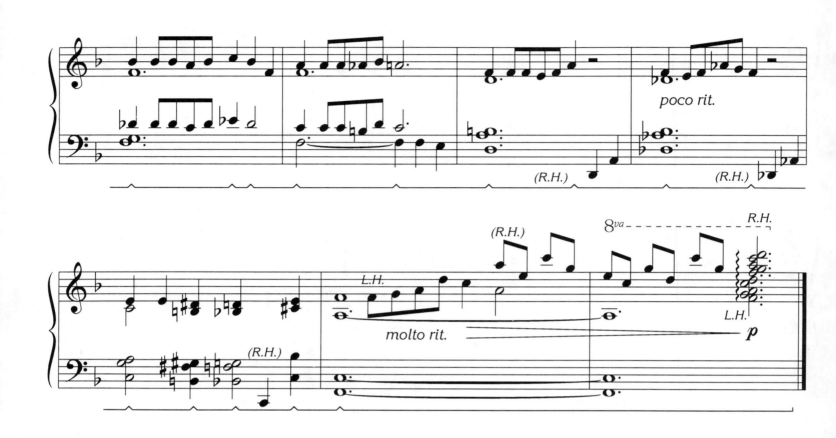

F Major (hands together)
(see Syllabus for metronomic requirement)

(hands together)

Root
Pos.   I   IV   I   V₇ I
            or V

Hide and Seek

Wynn-Anne Rossi

(Modal: No IMMT Required)

Novelette

Carol Klose

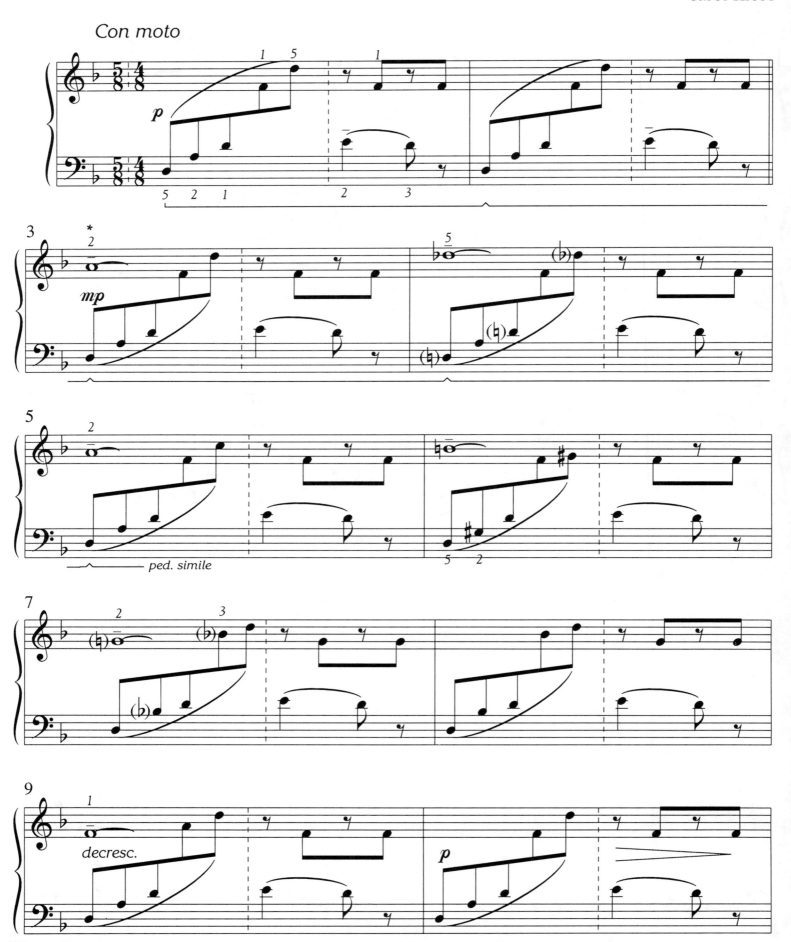

10 ∗ 𝄾 = *Hold note for nine beats.*

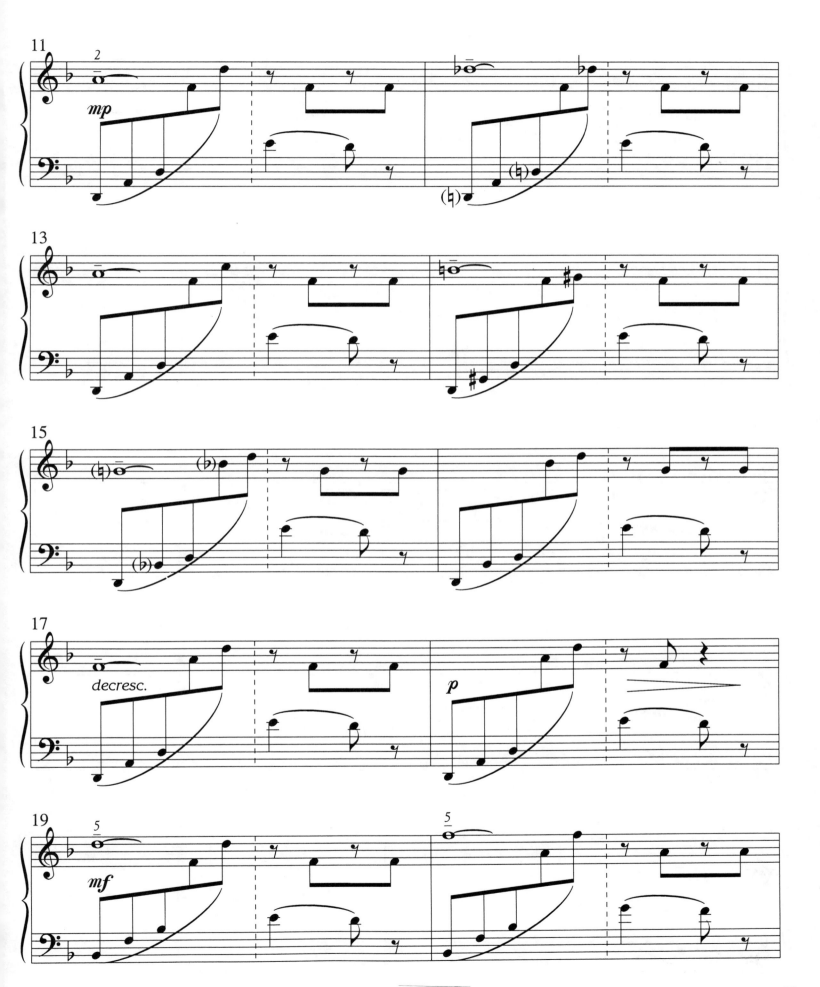

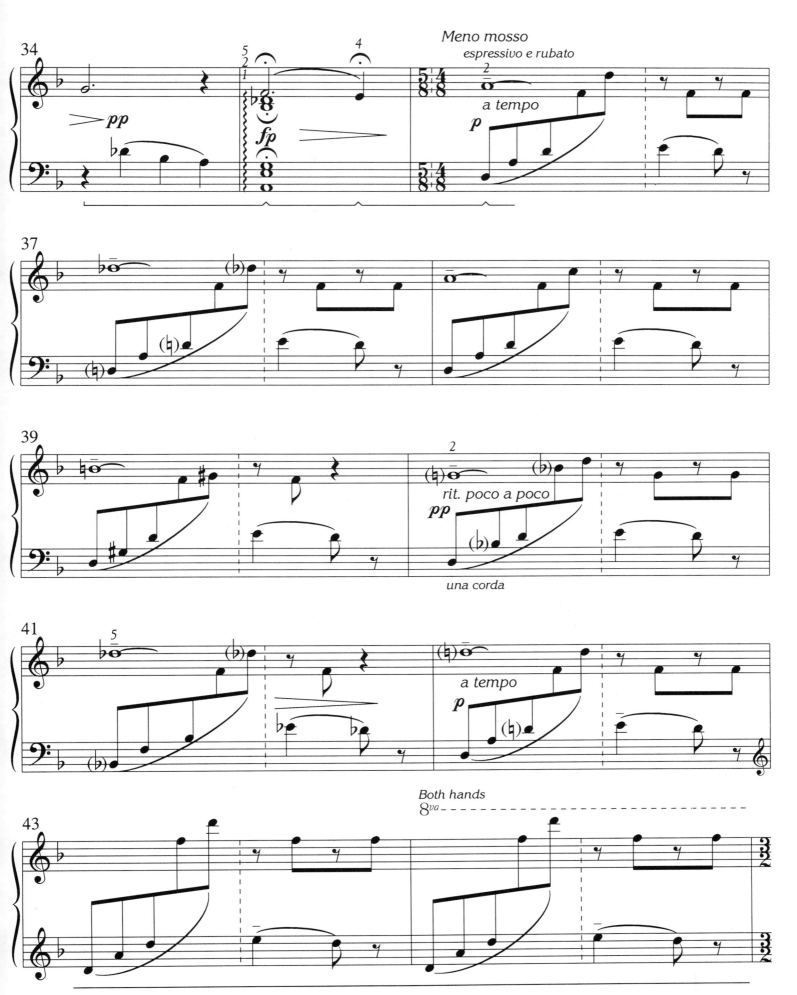

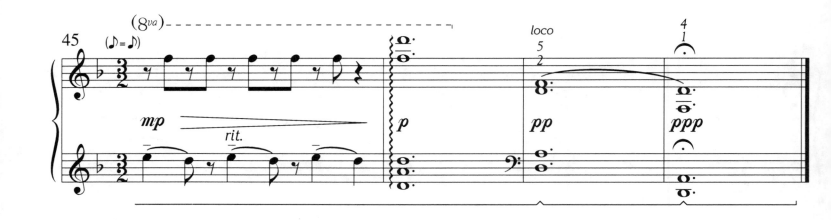

Les Oiseaux et Le Chat

"The Birds and the Cat"

Carol Klose

Con molto delicatezza e fantasìa (♩=168)

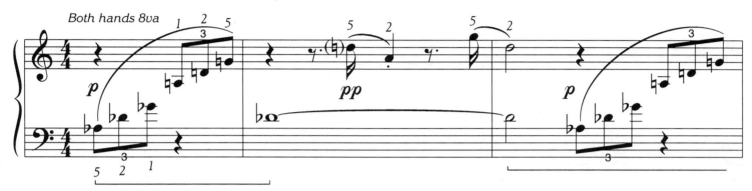

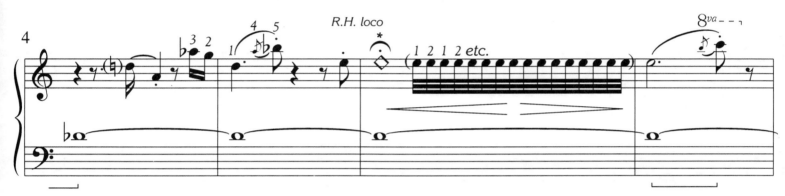

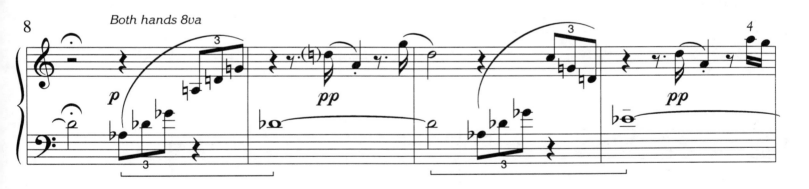

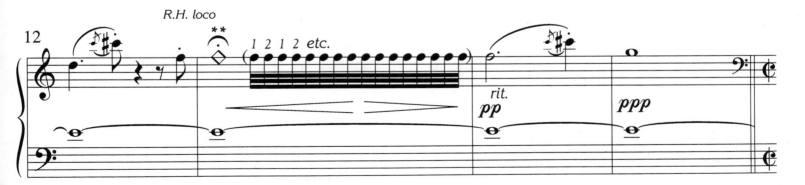

* Play ad lib repeated notes on E to imitate twittering bird-chatter.

** Play ad lib repeated notes on F.

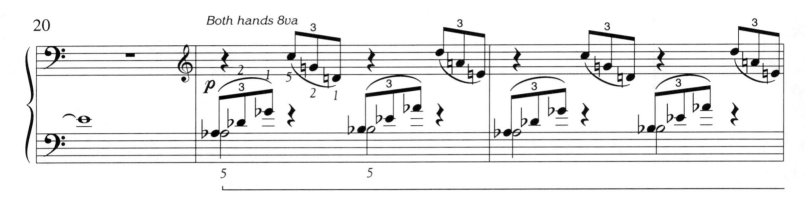

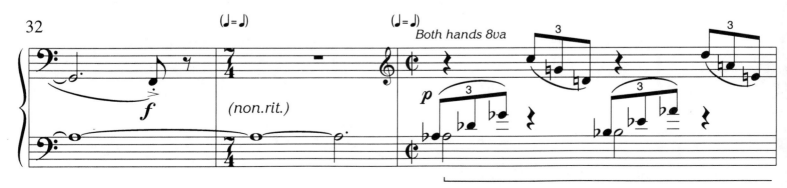

* Hold L.H. A-flat, allow overtones to ring, then depress damper pedal.

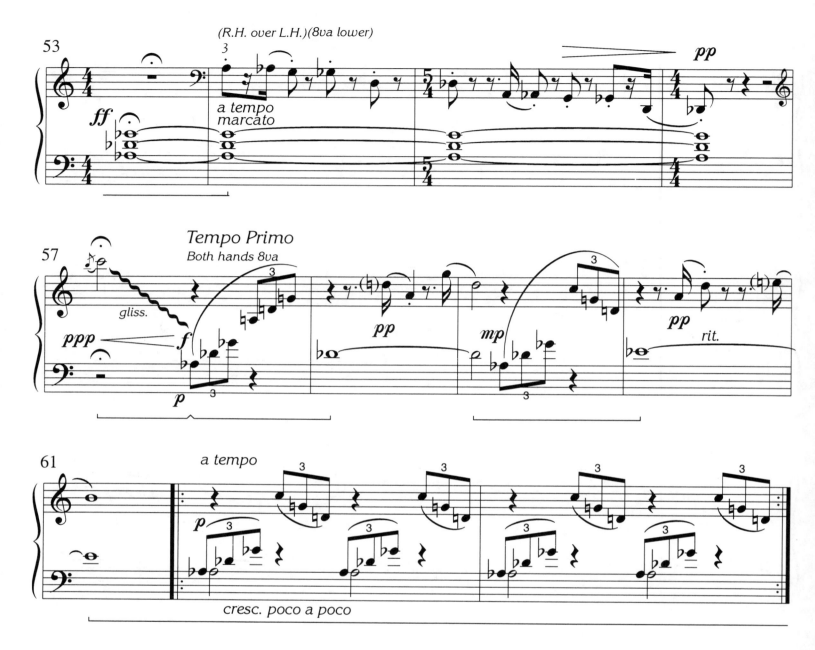

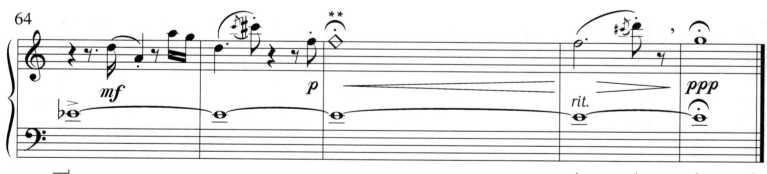

** *Play ad lib repeated notes on F.*

(Modal: No IMMT Required)

Reverie

for Kimberly Blair Condron

Eugénie R. Rocherolle

* pedal on 1st & 3rd beats unless otherwise indicated

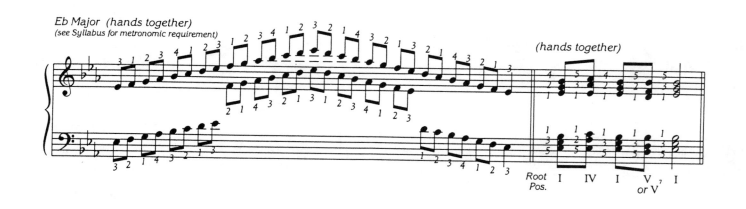

To Emily Schmitz

Epitaph

(The Rainforest Remembers)

Carol Klose

At a slow steady tempo, with foreboding (♩=66)

(Modal: No IMMT Required)

Remembering

Patricia W. King

27

Wedding Day
In The Royal Gardens Of Tokyo

Andante moderato

Carol Klose

31

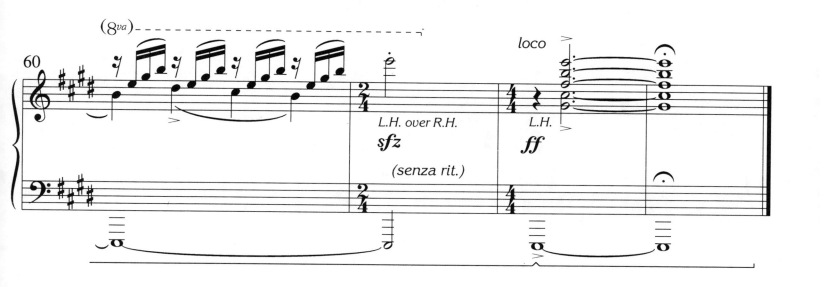

Oshkosh Toccata

To the students of Sara Bradley Mason

Carol Klose

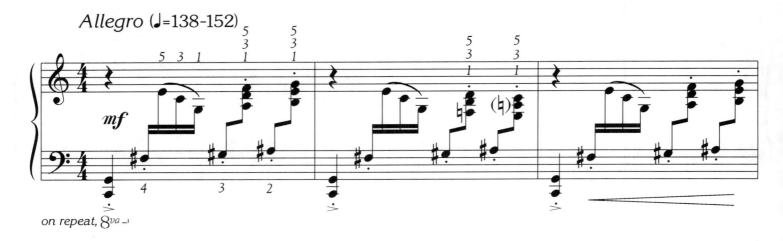

C Major (hands together)
(see Syllabus for metronomc requirement)

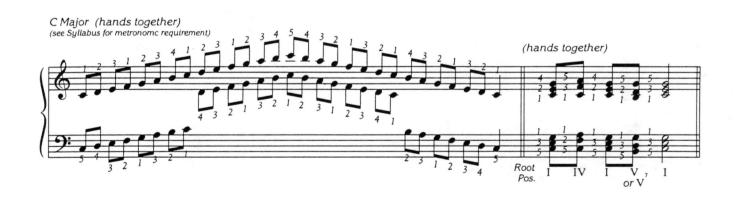

MUSICIANSHIP PHASES
IE Classification
(Fingerings are suggestions, not requirements)

Scales: (hands together)

(see syllabus for metromomic marking)

(majors)

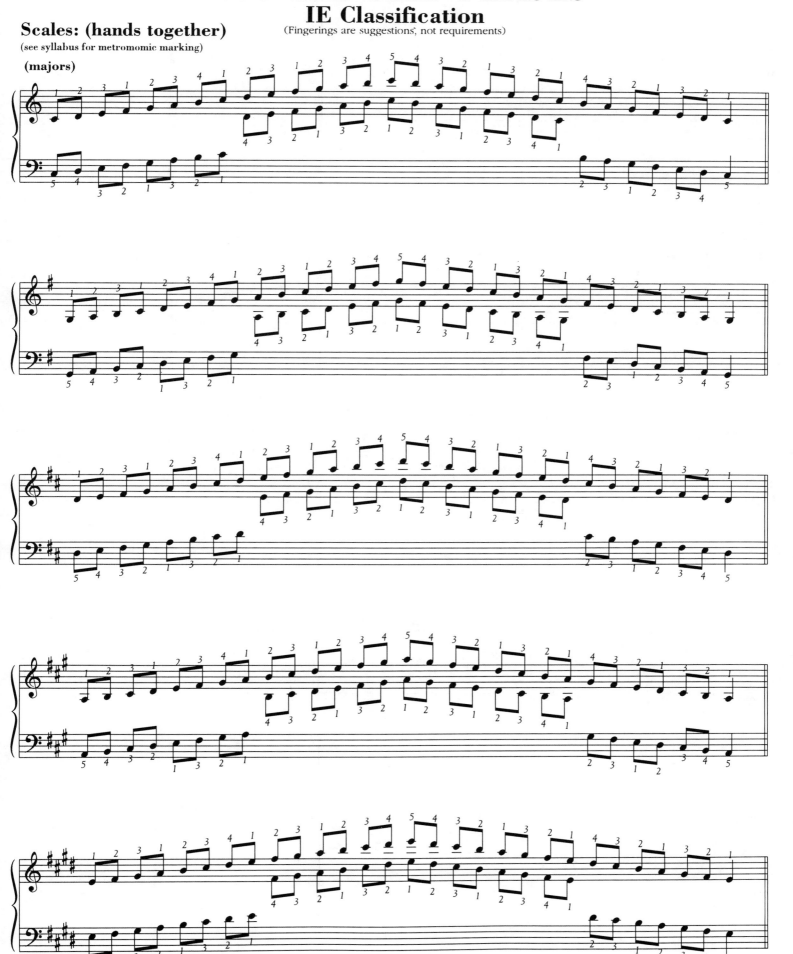

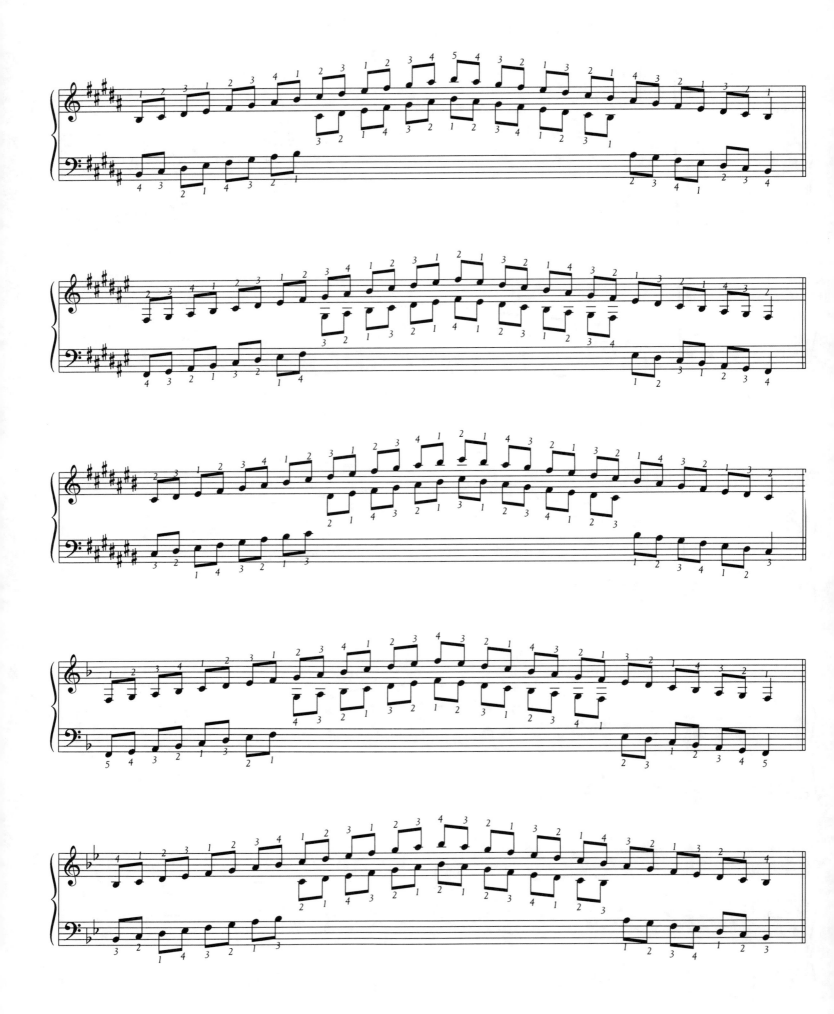

45

(harmonic minors)

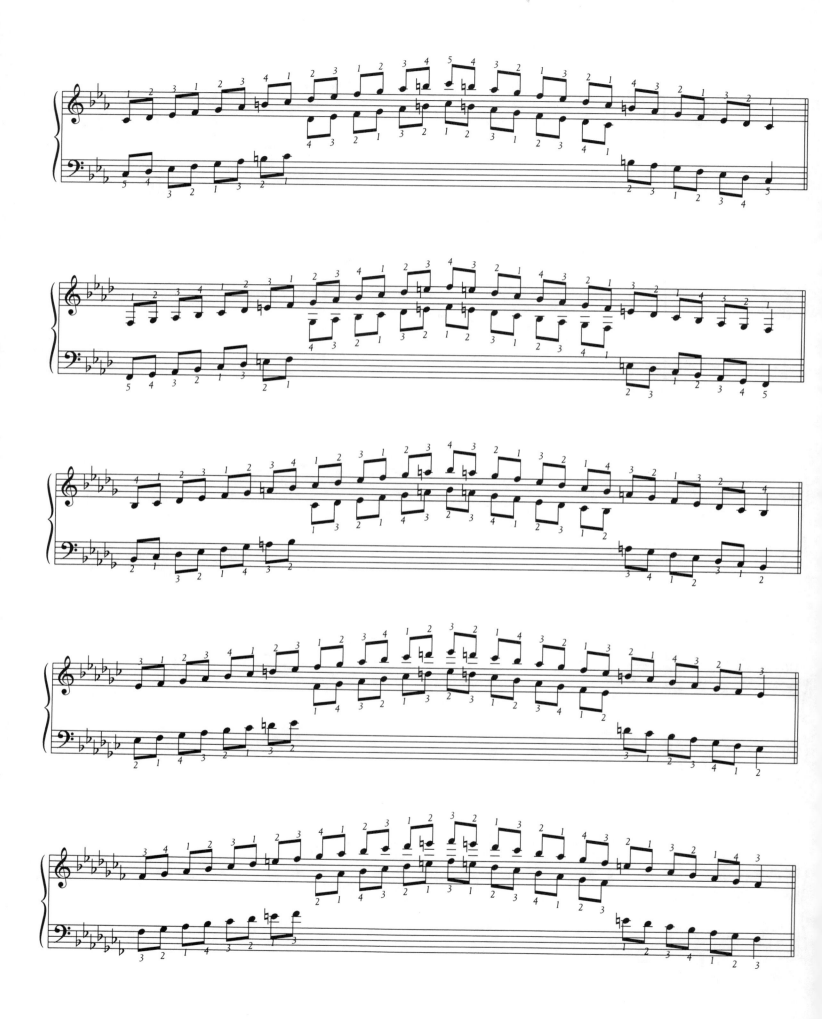

(melodic minors)

49

Chords: (separately or together)

(Majors)

(minors)

(diminished)

Root 1st. 2nd.
Pos. Inv. Inv.

(augmented)

Root 1st. 2nd.
Pos. Inv. Inv.

Cadences: (hands together)

(Majors)

Root Pos.   I   IV   I   V₇   I
         or V

(minors)

Root Pos.   i   iv   i   V₇   i
          or V

Arpeggios: (hands together)

(see Syllabus for metronomic requirement)

(Majors)

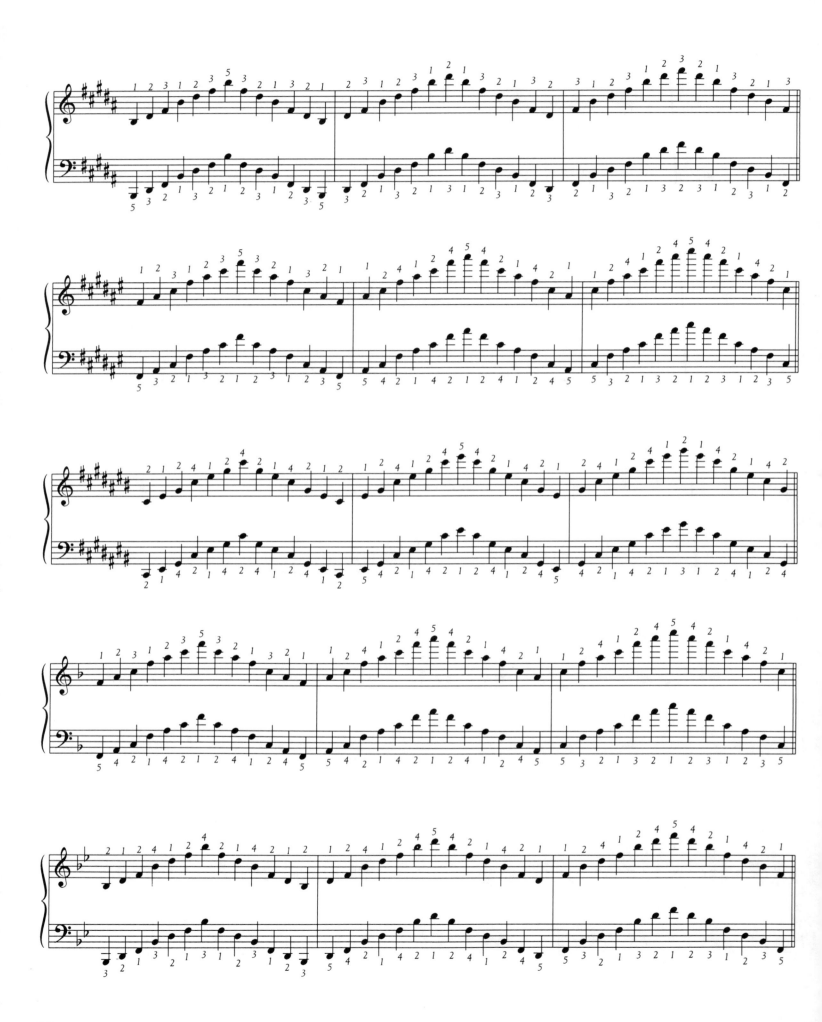

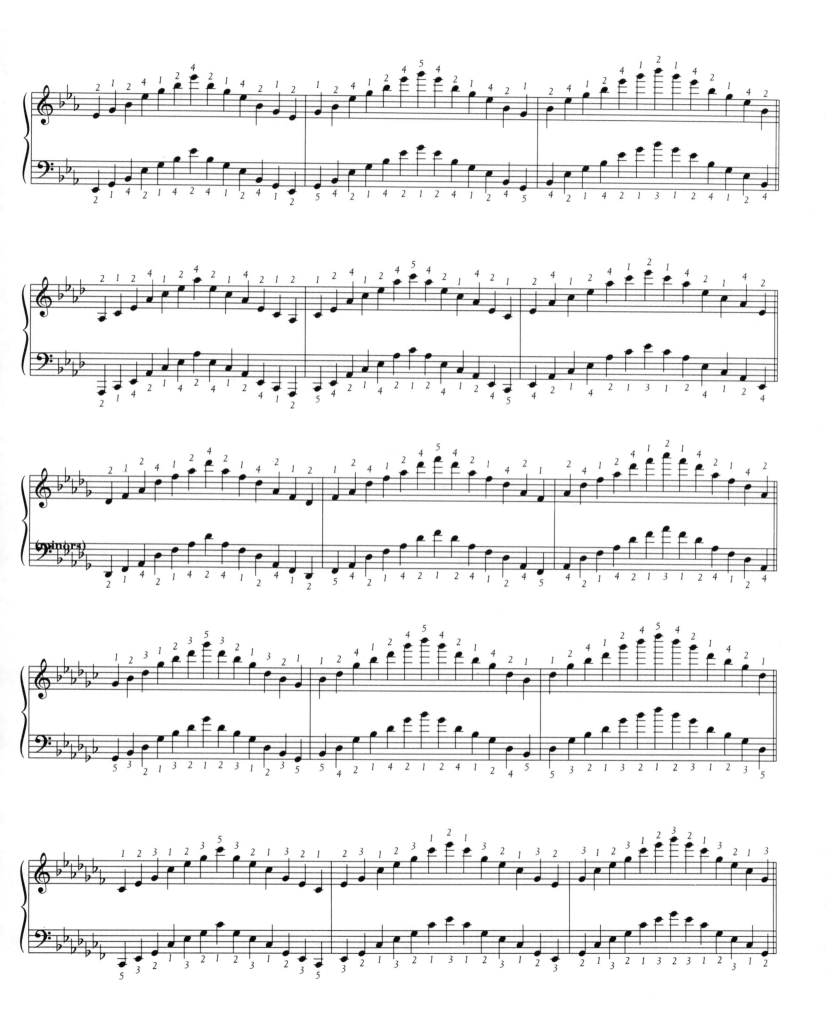

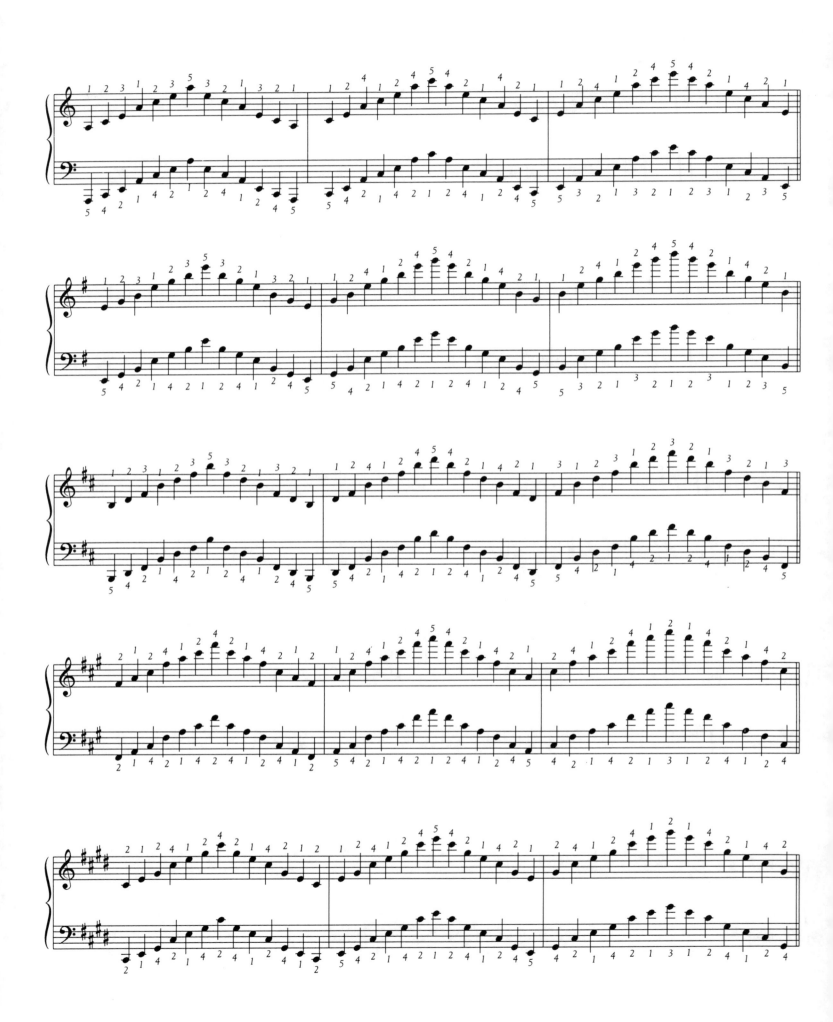

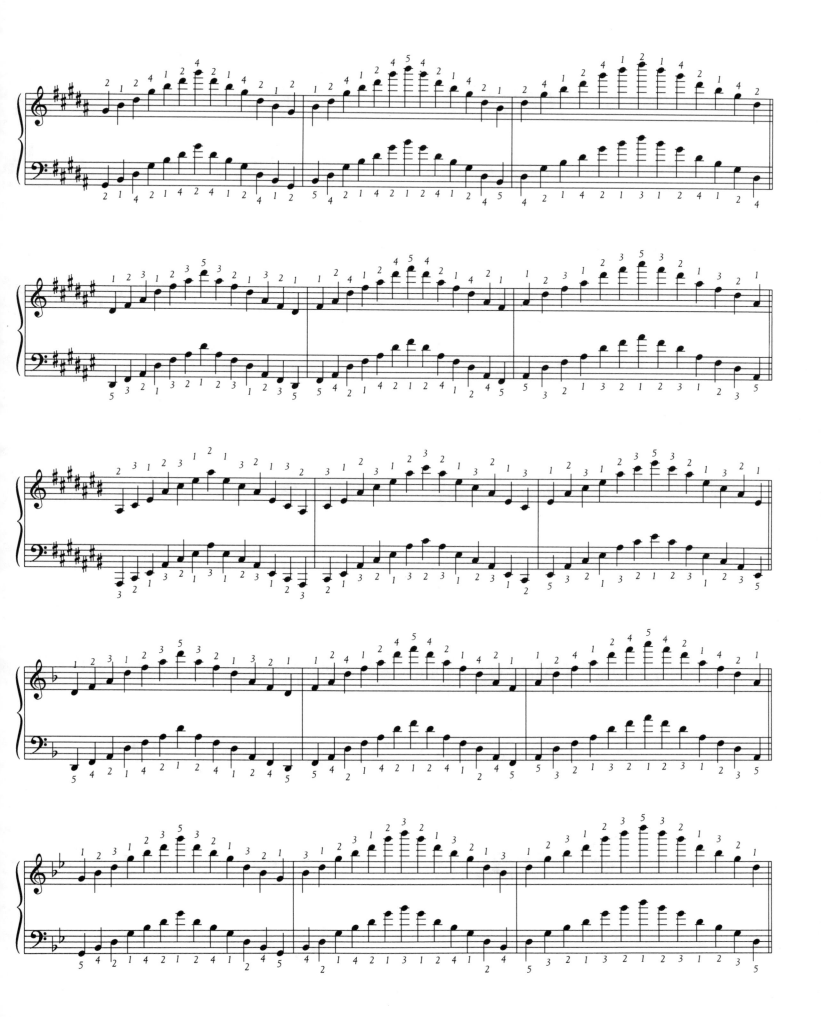

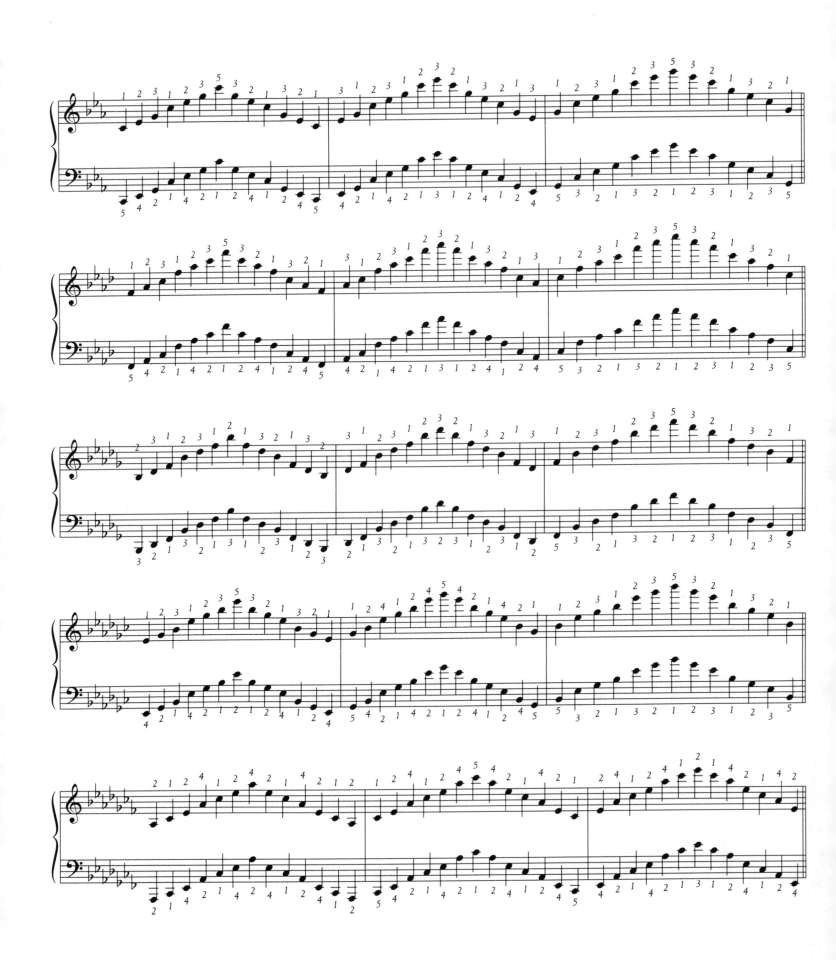

See the Guild Syllabus for additional Phases:
Ear Training, Transposition,
Improvisation, and Sight-Reading.

IF Classification

Scales: (hands together)
(see syllabus for metromomic marking)

(majors)

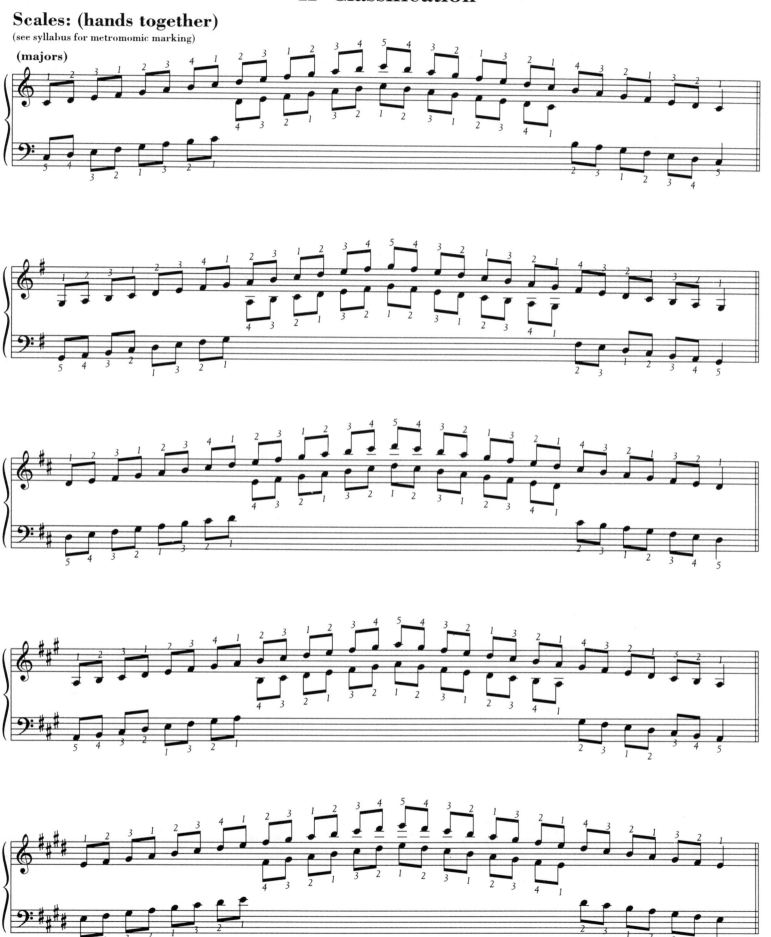

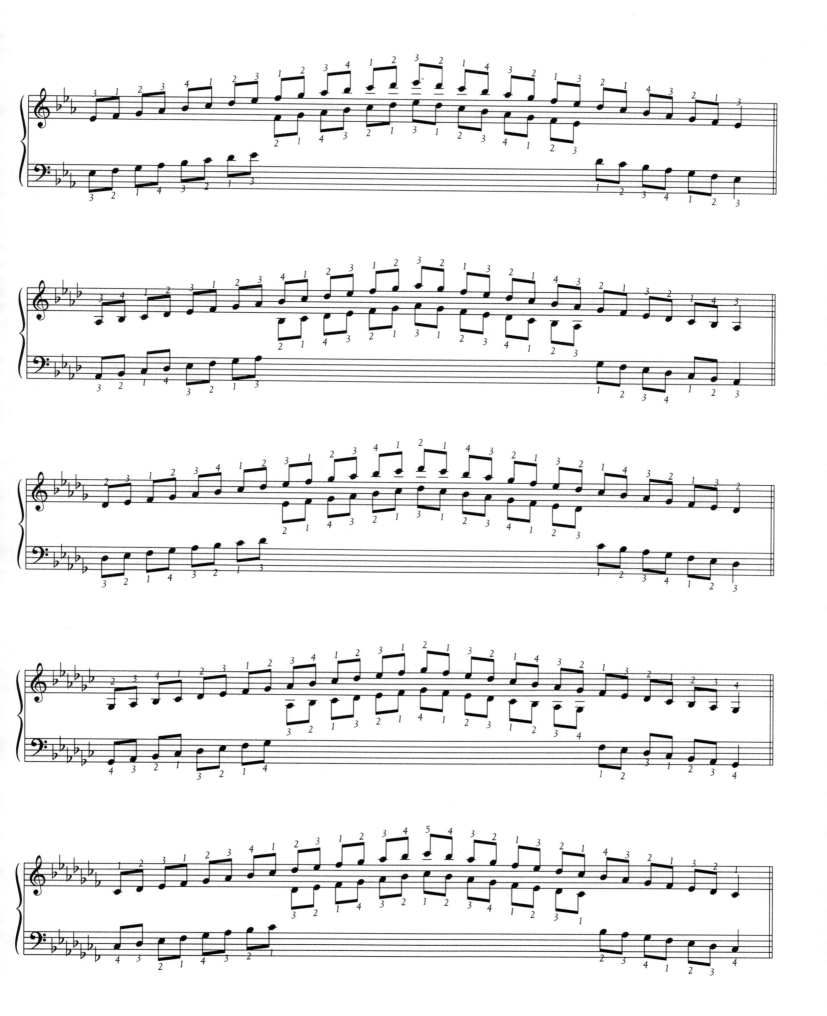

(harmonic minors)

64

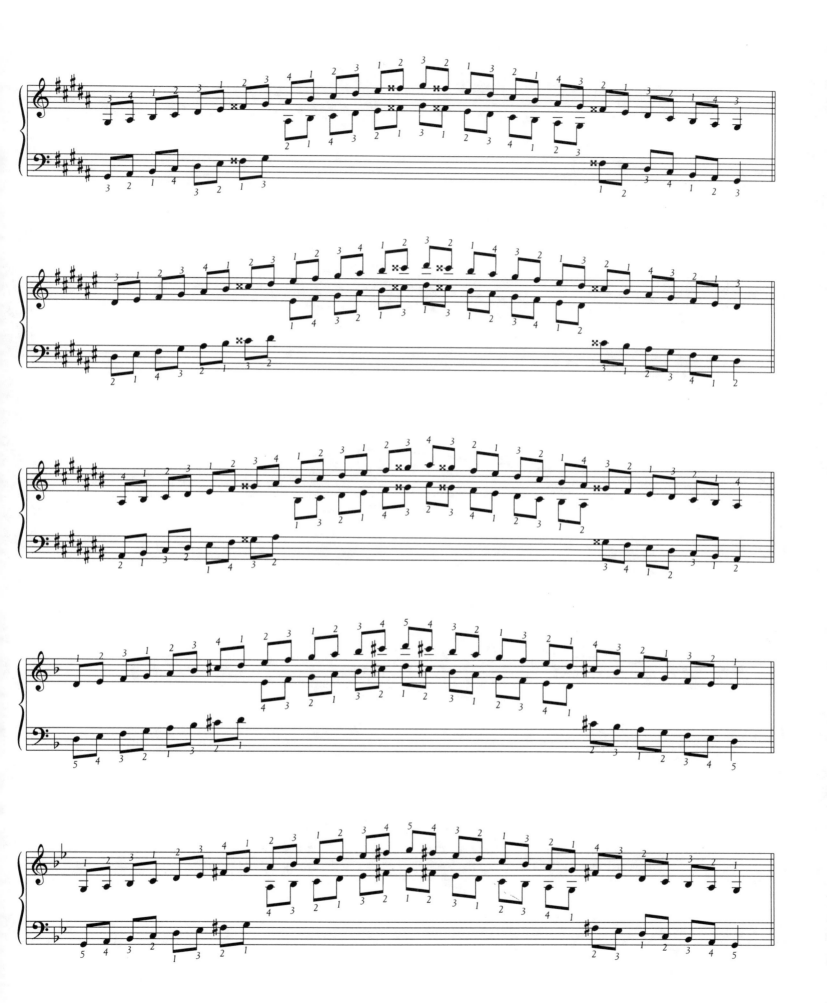

67

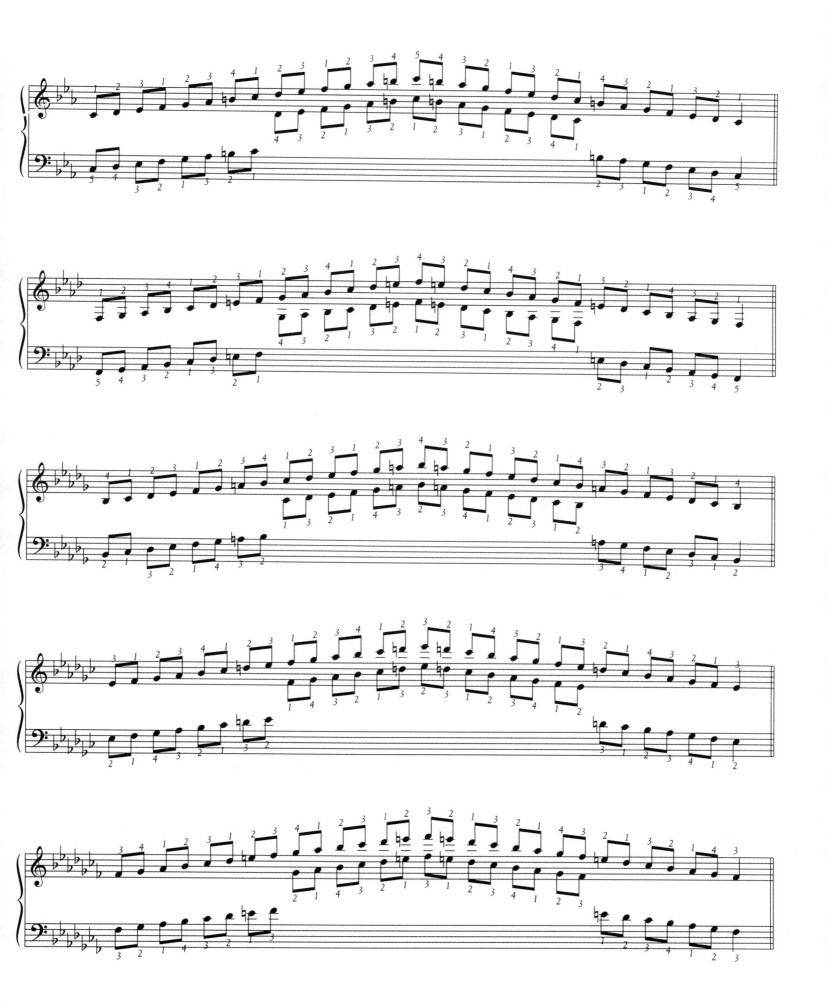

Chords: (hands together)

(Majors)

(minors)

Cadences: (hands together)

(Majors)

Arpeggios: (hands together)

(see Syllabus for metronomic requirement)

(Majors)

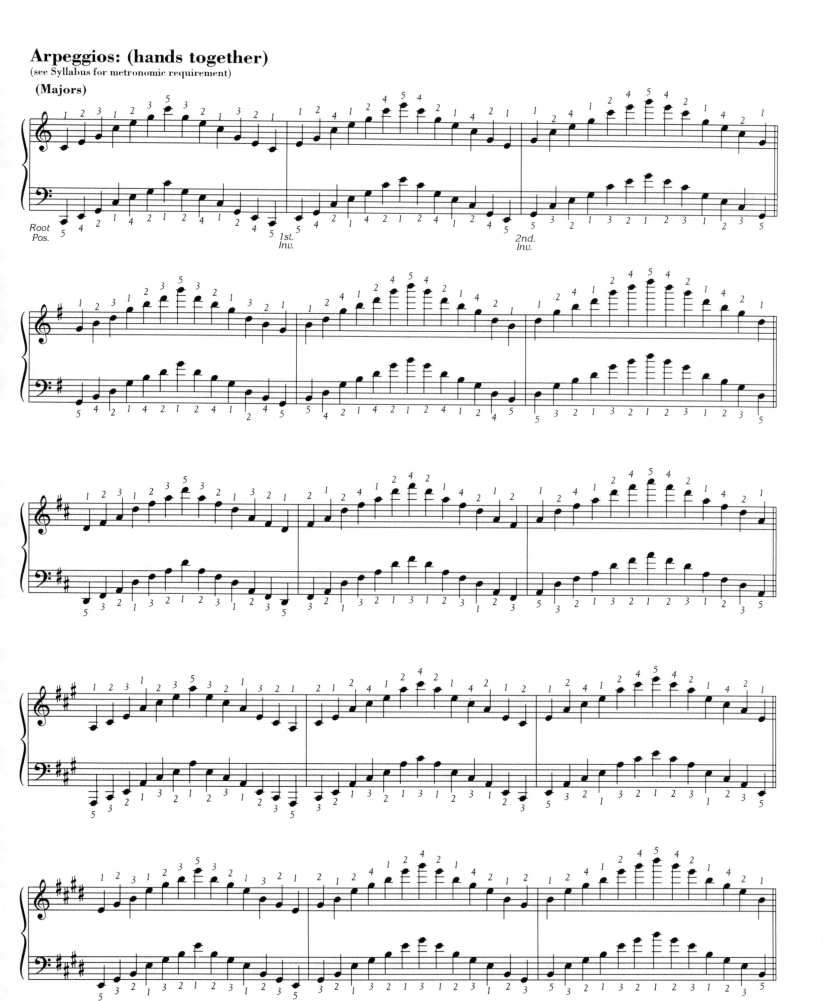

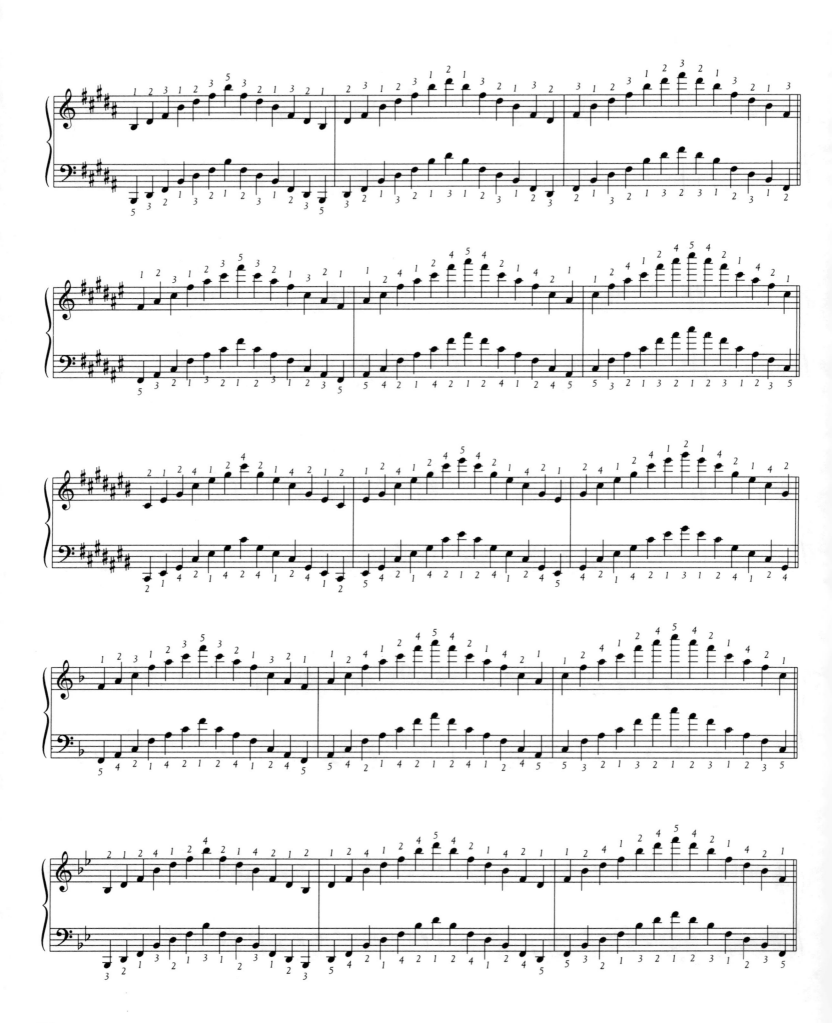

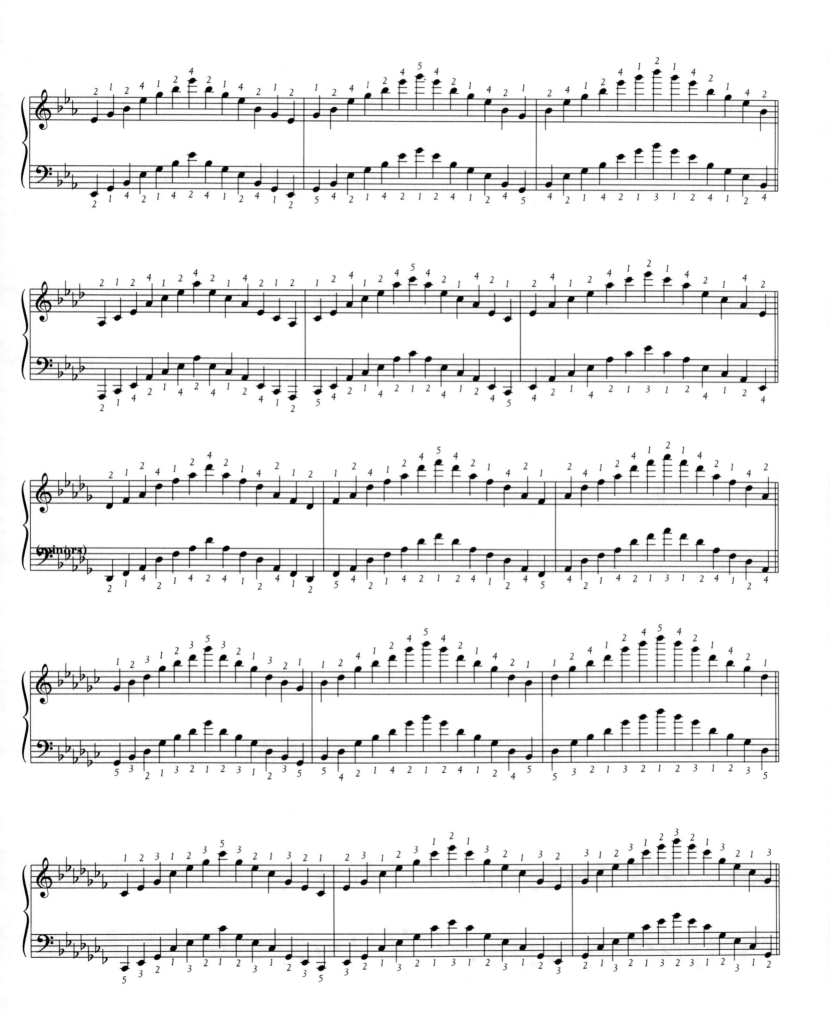

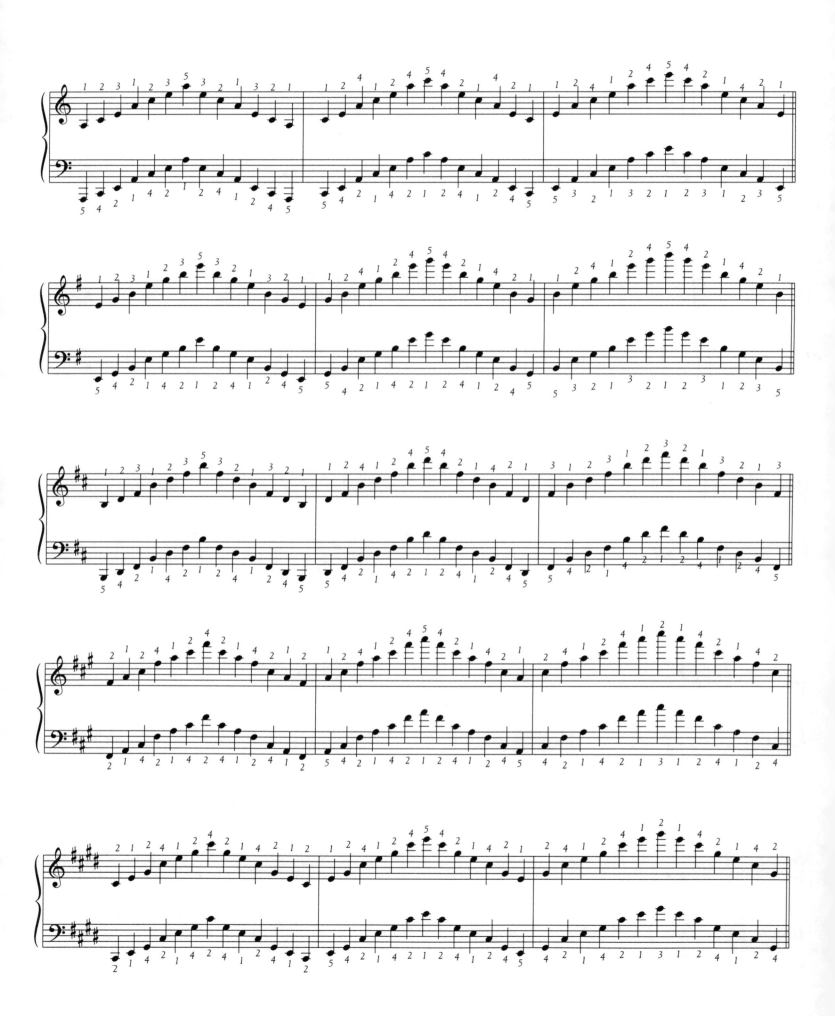

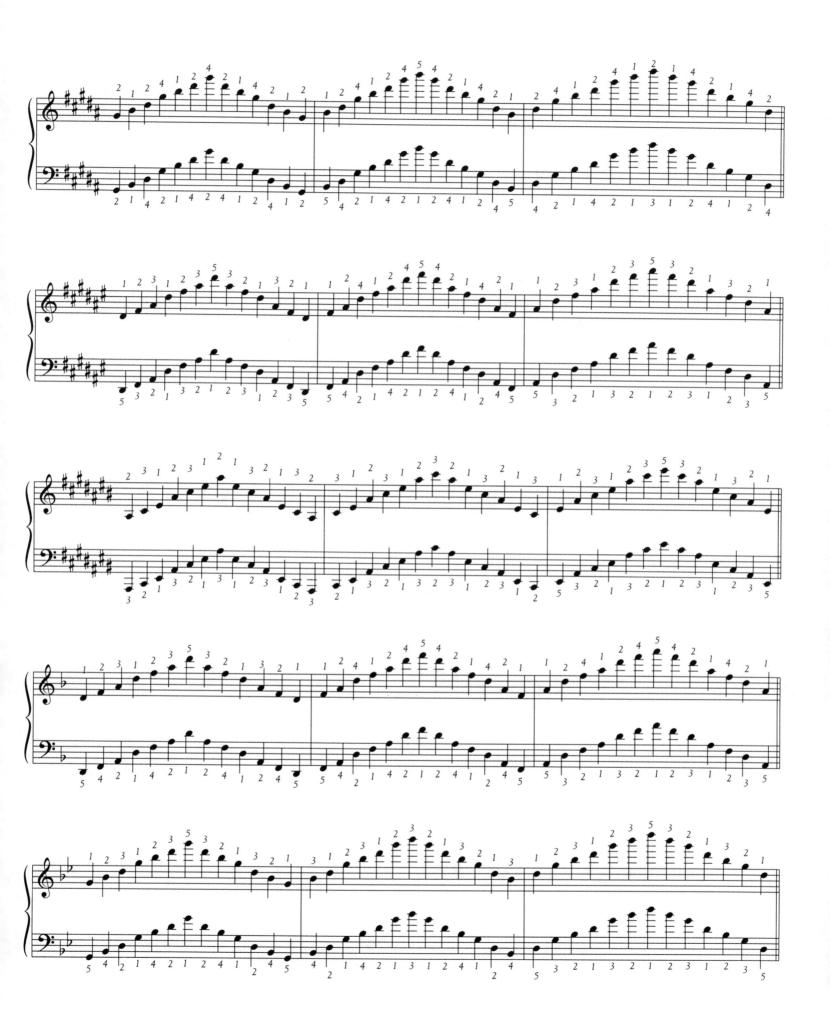

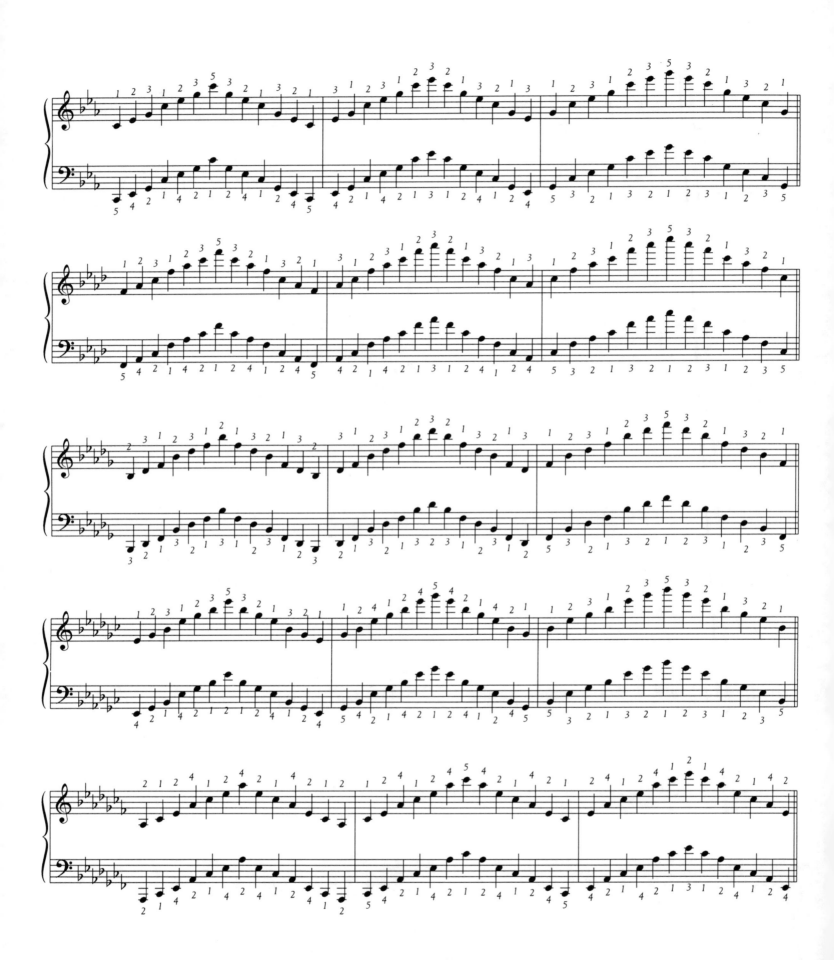

See the Guild Syllabus for additional Phases:
Ear Training, Transposition,
Improvisation, and Sight-Reading.

TEACHER'S NOTES:

TEACHER'S NOTES: